Original title:
The Orchid Observer

Copyright © 2025 Creative Arts Management OÜ
All rights reserved.

Author: Levi Montgomery
ISBN HARDBACK: 978-1-80566-767-4
ISBN PAPERBACK: 978-1-80566-837-4

Beyond the Blossoms

In a garden where flowers scheme,
Roses plot, and daisies dream.
But here comes a bee, buzzing loud,
Crashing through petals, feeling proud.

Laughter echoes from leaf to leaf,
A butterfly snickers, sharing grief.
"Stay off my turf!" the tulips shout,
While the sun just grins, no doubt.

What's that smell from the clover patch?
A pastry thief, a cunning match!
The daisies joke, "Can't trust a bee,"
As they sip nectar, gaily free.

But in the twist of nature's tune,
The gnome reveals a charming rune.
Says, "Play nice under the sun's beam,
Life's much funnier than it may seem!"

Orchids Underfoot

Orchids prance upon the floor,
Chatting secrets, wanting more.
"Have you heard about that lace?"
Spill the tea in blooming grace.

Down below, some roots are crass,
Spilling tales about the grass.
"Don't trust that worm, he's twice a cheat,
He just raided our dinner treat!"

The tulips giggle, paint their tales,
As the daisies join with flailing tails.
"Watch your petals!" they squeal with glee,
A puppy's coming, oh dear me!

Beneath the sun, they sway and play,
Each bloom with quirks, in bright array.
But alas, when dusk begins to creep,
They all pretend they're fast asleep!

An Observer's Garden Tales

A garden gnome with monocle fine,
Observes the chaos, sipping wine.
"Why do the daisies dance so wild?
They must think they're a blooming child!"

Toadstools whisper, keep it discreet,
As the lily pads tap their feet.
"A waltz of frogs, what a fine sight,
They croak and leap in sheer delight!"

Bumblebees throw a clumsy bash,
As they stumble, buzzing with a crash.
While the thistles poke with a laugh,
"Careful now, don't make them chaff!"

But amidst the mirth and joyful jest,
Old roots claim, "We're truly blessed!"
In soil rich, this garden sings,
Where laughter grows on floral wings!

Whispers of Petals

In a garden where giggles bloom,
Petals whisper secrets of doom.
Bees wear tiny hats, oh so bright,
Dancing 'round flowers, what a sight!

A butterfly in slippers prances,
While ladybugs join in the dances.
The tulips chuckle, what a scene,
As daisies play peek-a-boo, so keen!

Each stem is a stand-up in its prime,
Telling jokes about the sun's sweet chime.
Laughter echoes with every gust,
In this floral realm, it's a must!

So come take a stroll on this path,
Where flora ignites happy laughs.
In nature's circus, oh so grand,
Plants hold the punchlines, isn't it grand?

Beneath the Violet Veil

Beneath a sky so rich and blue,
Violets gossip about much ado.
A clownish gnome with a floppy hat,
Rides on a snail—imagine that!

Hummingbirds with shades of green,
Skydiving down, a funny scene.
They tickle the petals, make them blush,
In this wild world, there's never a hush.

Roses roll over in fits of mirth,
Counting their thorns as a sign of worth.
Dahlias play cards, bluff with style,
Winning hearts all the while!

Oh, join the fun, it's never stale,
Under this sweet violet veil.
Where nature's joy is a lively dance,
And laughter grows with every chance!

An Elegy for Blooming Grace

Oh, dear blooms that dance in the sun,
Falling like jokes, each laugh's begun.
Tulips in tuxedos, strutting about,
While daisies tease with a playful shout.

Petals droop down, it's quite a sight,
Cucumbers in gowns say, 'All's right!'
Ferns wave their fronds, calling a cheer,
As wacky weeds sing songs we all hear.

In corners, the violets throw a bash,
Drinking dew and munching on grass.
They tell tall tales of the skies above,
And tickle the wind with laughter and love.

An elegy penned not of sorrow's might,
But of giggles and wiggles, a pure delight.
Come share a chuckle, don't hesitate,
In this garden of laughter, it's never too late!

Silhouettes in Sunlight

In the light where shadows play so sly,
Flowers stretch out, like a wink and a sigh.
Sunflowers pose with their heads so high,
While daisies giggle, oh me, oh my!

Butterflies with pencils write their tales,
Of swaying grasses and windy gales.
The larkspur dreams of heights unknown,
While tulips argue who's a champion grown.

In this silly ballet of colors and shades,
Even the daffodils join the parades.
Swaying and swishing, they dance so bold,
With petals like laughter in the sun's warm gold.

So step right in, don't be shy,
In a world where the blooms laugh, we can't deny:
That life's a carnival, a zesty flight,
In these silhouettes, our hearts take flight!

Notes from the Blossoming World

In gardens where blossoms dance with glee,
A bee wore a hat, sipping on tea.
He sipped from a flower, tipped his fat brim,
And shouted, "This nectar's positively prim!"

Amidst blooms so colorful, antics abound,
A petal performed, not making a sound.
With laughter and cheer, the insects all pranced,
In a waltz of the flowers, they happily danced.

Interludes Among Orchids

Among the orchids, a snail took a dive,
Claiming, "I'm speedy!" The crowd was alive.
But as he crawled slowly, a crow took a glance,
And chuckled, "Oh dear, you've got no chance!"

A clumsy old moth just tripped on a stem,
Yelling, "I swear, I'm a flower, not him!"
The petals all giggled, swaying with pride,
As nature's own jesters continued their ride.

The Lure of the Exotic

An exotic bloom, bright and quite strange,
Flirted with bees, causing quite the exchange.
With colors so wild, it twirled and it spun,
Declaring, "Dear friends, let's all have some fun!"

Then came a critter, with dreams of a snack,
Thinking, "These petals are perfect to hack!"
But the flower just giggled, puffed out its chest,
"I bloom for your laughter, I'm truly the best!"

Awakened with Blossoms

With dawn breaking softly, the blossoms all yawned,
A lizard on guard, pretending to fawn.
"I'm the king of this patch, the ruler of cheer!"
Said the daisies, "Oh really? We've ruled for a year!"

Then came a butterfly, full of delight,
"I've got some bright wings; I'm ready to flight!"
But tangled in silk, it began to complain,
Twirling through petals, it laughed through the pain.

Tapestry of Nature's Lullaby

In the garden, blooms a tale,
With petals bright, they never pale.
Bees wear glasses for the show,
While butterflies dance to and fro.

Sunlight spills like syrup thick,
Worms on stilts, they make us tick.
Rainy clouds bring their own cheer,
They gossip, oh so loud and clear.

Squirrels debate on acorn finds,
While flowers plot their sneaky kinds.
A daisy winks, the roses laugh,
Nature's wit is quite the craft.

Amidst the leaves, a joke unfolds,
As petals share their secret holds.
All in harmony, they roll and play,
Nature's jesters in bright array.

Floral Musings

Tulips wear hats in the spring,
While daisies belt out tunes to sing.
Petunias recite their lines in style,
With every bloom, they raise a smile.

A cactus tried to join the fun,
But poked the jokes till they were done.
Sunflowers twirl, with heads held high,
Claiming the title of the sky.

Bumblebees boast with all their might,
Competing who can make the best flight.
Pansies giggle at the scene,
While violets plan a dance routine.

As colors clash in vibrant hues,
Nature's laughter never skews.
In this patch, we find delight,
Floral musings take their flight.

The Art of Stillness

A flower sits in thoughtful pose,
With roots that ponder, where it grows.
Chillin' in the breeze's sway,
Ignoring all that comes their way.

A tulip thinks it's quite a star,
While snails ascend from near and far.
Sunlight winks, a gentle tease,
To petals curled with evening ease.

Bamboo grass makes quiet bets,
On who can sway without regrets.
A lily dreams of quiet streams,
And smiles softly at moonbeams.

Innocence blooms in every shade,
As stillness chuckles at the parade.
Laughter rests beneath the trees,
Where nature sighs and takes its ease.

Echoes of Delicacy

Whispers float on gentle air,
As petals break out in a dare.
Tiny saplings try to race,
While elder trees just shake their case.

A ladybug with polka spots,
Claims it knows all the best plots.
Mushrooms giggle in bright hues,
With pals who choose the silliest views.

The breeze teases with light taps,
While crickets share their funny maps.
In nature's play, we find our spark,
Echoes of laughs in the dark.

With every bloom, a tale unfolds,
Of joy and quirk that nature holds.
Each delicate whisper carries glee,
In this garden, we're all carefree.

A Symphony of Color

In gardens bright, a dance unfolds,
With petals swaying, stories told.
A bee with rhythm, moves to the beat,
Sipping sweet nectar, oh what a treat!

Colors clash like a wild parade,
Dandelions envy the grand charade.
With every hue, laughter weaves,
As nature chuckles, and mischief leaves.

The sun looks on with a glimmering grin,
As flowers gossip, let the fun begin!
A clematis twirls, a daisy just laughs,
In this flowery world, joy surely staffs.

So join the fun in this vibrant play,
Where flora friends celebrate each day.
With colors bold and humor bright,
A symphony of laughter taking flight!

Secret Lives of Flora

If flowers could talk, oh what they'd say,
Whispering secrets in their own way.
The tulip giggles at the rose's plight,
While violets plot a playful little bite.

The lilacs plan a floral raid,
Sneaking up on birds and bees, unafraid.
"Let's dress the pond in petals anew!"
The willow smirks, "Oh, what fun we'll do!"

Sunlight gives a wink, as shadows sway,
Creating tales of mischief every day.
Leaves conceal, then burst out in cheer,
While roots conspire from far and near.

So roam the gardens, and take a look,
At the petals' whispers and how they cook.
An undercover play, where all can see,
The secret lives of flora, oh what glee!

Veins of Velvet

In the forest deep, with velvet veins,
Leaves tell tales with whimsical gains.
A fuchsia flair and a gossiping spruce,
Chortling softly, with humor acute.

"Watch me sway!" cried the luscious fern,
"While all the flowers take their turn."
A petal prances, a berry rolls,
While grass blades chuckle, playing their roles.

The wind joins in with a boisterous laugh,
As vines braid jokes like a craftsman's craft.
Twisting and turning in glorious spree,
Nature's delight, unbounded and free.

So embrace the green with a sprinkle of fun,
Where life is a show and joy's never done.
With veins of velvet, and laughter so spry,
In this garden of quirk, let your spirit fly!

Echoes of Exotic Beauty

In the realm of blooms, a wild affair,
Exotic whispers fill the air.
A cactus winks with a prickly jest,
While orchids strut, all dressed to impress.

"Can you believe?" says a bold marigold,
"Last week's rain was like liquid gold!"
The hibiscus chuckles with each passing breeze,
Teasing the roses with a snarky tease.

Laughter cascades from the trees so tall,
As flames of color get ready to sprawl.
Petals parade, with antics galore,
In this circus of flora, who could ask for more?

So step right up to this beautiful show,
Where the echoes of blooms make feelings grow.
Exotic beauty wraps us in mirth,
In this joyous dance, we find our worth!

Reflections of a Blooming Mind

In the garden, a thought peeked,
I tripped over roots while I winked.
The bees wore shades, feeling cool,
While I slipped, looking like a fool.

Petals giggled, tickled by breeze,
Waving hello, with such ease.
A butterfly danced in the air,
I swatted, but my aim was just flair.

Tangled vines whispered soft tales,
Of mishaps where laughter prevails.
I pondered blooms, wisdom so bright,
Yet fell in the mud, much to my delight.

With each bee buzzing, a chuckle grew,
In this patch of green, hilarity flew.
I strolled 'neath a sunflower's grin,
Admitting, the laughter was where I win.

The Eye of the Bloom

In a garden where petals sigh,
A tulip watched as I walked by.
With a wink, it whispered low,
"What's that on your shoe? A garden toe?"

Sunbeams laughed, casting shadows wide,
While I checked where my big toe tried to hide.
Lilies giggled, swaying with glee,
As I tripped on a leaf, oh dear me!

Dandelions chuckled, full of fluff,
Saying my rhymes were definitely rough.
"Hey there, do you sing, or just hum?"
With flowers mocking, I felt quite dumb.

But camaraderie bloomed all around,
As I danced with weeds, both slippery and brown.
Enjoying the humor, I found my stride,
In the realm of blooms, I took it all in pride.

Amongst Fragile Harvests

In a patch where zucchinis twirl,
I spotted a sneeze from a strange little girl.
She giggled and pointed, what a surprise,
As I dodged raindrops from cloudy skies.

Lavenders whispered, scents so sweet,
While I attempted to keep my feet neat.
But mud splashed like a paintbrush's thrill,
As petals laughed, an uproar they did instill.

A scarecrow danced, not minding the show,
With crows as his audience, they'd never know.
My shoes were pastels, splattered with flair,
I joined in the dance, without any care.

Harvests stumbled in the light's gleam,
Ripe tomatoes giggled, living the dream.
In this garden of folly, I found my home,
Embracing the laughter that makes me feel grown.

Garden of Tranquility

Among blossoms where the fragrance is bold,
I met a cat who was rather old.
He purred at the daisies, claiming his throne,
As I sat nearby, feeling quite alone.

But daisies whispered, "Join in the fun,"
While a plump little robin enjoyed the sun.
I told them my tales, a jester with flair,
They chuckled and chirped, filling the air.

With weeds chiming in, the jokes flowed like wine,
"Your shade is quite lovely, but please don't recline!"
As I rolled in the grass, I felt such a buzz,
Even flowers know joy's the ultimate fuzz.

In this tranquil garden, goofiness thrives,
Where laughter erupts and each moment derives,
I bask in the whimsy that fills up my heart,
In a patch of absurdity, I play my part.

Secrets in the Greenhouse

Behind the glass, what secrets hide,
A squirrel in a pot, oh, what a ride!
Leaves gossip louder than you might think,
Sipping on water, or perhaps a drink.

Gnomes play cards, their laughter loud,
While daisies and tulips form a crowd.
The sun's a bard, telling tales so bright,
Of snails with dreams of soaring flight.

Kooky plants wear hats, all mismatched styles,
Chasing each other in playful miles.
A cactus teases with spiky glee,
Saying, "You'll prick yourself; just wait and see!"

In this jungle, fun unfolds,
With plant-filled stories yet untold.
So peek inside, come join the spree,
And laugh with blooms so wild and free.

Silent Elegance

In quiet corners, neighbors live,
An orchid whispers, 'Please, no give!'
With petals prim, it sips on air,
While ferns roll dice, without a care.

A peacock struts, its plumage bright,
But in the shadow, blooms take flight.
"I'm more elegant!" the lilies claim,
While roses file a cheeky blame.

The silence cracks with laughter's tune,
As ivy trips with dancing moon.
The vines conspire in leafy jest,
So who's the fairest? They'll never rest!

Beneath this calm, a riot brews,
Unsuspecting eyes may miss the clues.
So tiptoe softly, hear the jest,
In silent elegance, all blooms are blessed.

An Ephemeral Dance

In twilight hours, the petals twirl,
A waltz of leaves, oh, what a whirl!
The moon, a spotlight, gleams just right,
While shadows sway in soft delight.

Grasshoppers join with jolly leaps,
While crickets serenade in peeps.
The daisies kick off their little shoes,
With laughter ringing through the hues.

A butterfly slips on fancy pants,
Declaring that it's time to dance!
And with each flutter, joy's bestowed,
In fragrant realms where smiles explode.

So step inside this garden spree,
Join in the fun, just you and me.
An ephemeral dance, let worries cease,
As blooms and bugs share joy and peace.

The Language of Blossoms

Whispers in petals, oh, what a thrill,
The cosmos giggles, it knows the drill.
"Hey there, sunflower, look up high!"
While violets wink, saying, "Just try!"

A daisy shouts, "I'm the queen of fun!"
While buttercups smile, enjoying the sun.
"Is that a peony? It's dressed to impress!"
But geraniums laugh, "What a crazy mess!"

Sass in the air, it's a plant-filled chat,
"Stop rolling, you rogue, it's not where you're at!"
The language of blossoms, a playful sound,
Where petals mingle, and joy is found.

So join the chorus in verdant hues,
Listen to the blooms, share their views.
In every leaf, let laughter gleam,
For in their chatter, we find our dream.

A Watcher's Quiet Reflection

In the garden, I take a seat,
While petals dance to a secret beat.
The bees gossip, a buzzing choir,
I swear they conspire, oh what a liar!

A butterfly flits, with dubious grace,
Its landing is often a comical chase.
I laugh at the ladybug's clumsy ballet,
Who knew insects had such a quirky display?

The flowers giggle, they seem to know,
That I'm a watcher, not just a show.
With a sip of tea, I'm feeling quite grand,
But I spill it all; oh, isn't life planned?

The garden's alive with a humorous dance,
I chuckle at blooms that just want their chance.
So here I remain, with laughter and peace,
In this silly world, my worries decrease.

Moonlit Whispers of Blooms

Under the stars, the petals glow bright,
They whisper secrets, oh what a sight!
An idle tulip calls out to me,
"Come join our party, it's wild and free!"

The roses discuss their fragrant attire,
While daisies giggle, their laughter won't tire.
The moon shrugs and joins in the fun,
An unexpected guest, she's outdone everyone!

The night is a canvas, painted with cheer,
With blossoms that wink, as if they know fear.
I trip on a charm, that's woven in vines,
And fall on the grass, where the laughter aligns.

This garden of jesters, such whimsical sights,
Where flowers plot scandals under soft lights.
So I'll keep my watch, with a grin on my face,
Embracing the chaos, this botanical space!

Embracing the Elegant

In a tuxedo, the lilies stand tall,
They sip on the dew, so regal, not small.
With petals like silk and a fragrance so grand,
They nod with a flair, like they own the whole land.

The daisies wear crowns, in their playful attire,
While saucy geraniums dance by the fire.
I can't help but giggle, such class in the air,
As the garden unfolds all its humorous flair.

The orchids look puzzled, what happened to pride?
As violets smirk from the nearby side.
Even the weeds wear their best for a laugh,
Trying to fit in, though they don't qualify for the staff.

So here's to the blooms, in their glamorous game,
Who turn up their petals and play without shame.
In the grand ballroom of nature, we twirl and we sway,
With laughter and joy, every night and day.

The Keeper of Botanical Secrets

In the whispers of leaves, a secret I hear,
The hydrangeas giggle, full of good cheer.
With butterflies winking, oh what a delight,
They plot their mischief under the moon's light.

The ferns flaunt their fronds, like they own the glen,
They claim to be wise, but are giggly again.
Each petal has stories, each leaf a tall tale,
Of squirrels in tuxes, and snails that regale.

"Why do you stare?" asks a bold little sprout,
"Join in the laughter, there's no need to pout!"
So I take a step closer, with much to behold,
As the garden shares laughter, a treasure of old.

The keeper of secrets, I promise to be,
To guard all these giggles, and joy without fee.
So here in this patch, I'll dance and I'll sing,
With every bloom's laughter, oh what joy they bring!

The Quiet Encounter

In a garden so still, under leaves so bright,
Two blooms had a chat, it was quite a sight.
One said, "I'm a petal, oh so refined,
While you get the bugs, I get the kind!"

With a laugh and a nod, the other replied,
"While you sip on dew, I've got nothing to hide.
They flock to my fragrance, they can't get enough,
Though my charms may seem clumsy, I'm quite the tough!"

The sun peeked in, giving warmth to the day,
The petals exchanged jokes in a flowery way.
"Your leaves are so green, but mine dance with flair,
If only we could swap, would you even dare?"

Underneath all the banter, a friendship did bloom,
In that quiet garden, they light up the gloom.
A bond built on laughter, no worry or fear,
Two flowers so silly, the best atmosphere!

Allure of the Unseen

In a patch of the wild, where shadows can play,
There lurked a shy blossom, in secret it lay.
"Come closer, dear friend, if you wish to see,
The beauty I'm hiding, oh just let it be!"

A passerby stopped, with a curious frown,
"What's so special about your silken crown?
I've seen blooms that shine, and scents that enthrall,
But you, sweet little thing, don't seem bright at all!"

The flower just chuckled, with petals quite meek,
"Sometimes it's silence that decides what we seek.
For every bright face, there's a whispering soul,
With charms that are subtle, and make us feel whole!"

Yet even in shadows, a trickster appears,
With cheeky little pollen that dances with cheers.
So next time you wander, in gardens so green,
Remember the magic of that which unseen!

Chronicles of the Green

Oh gather around, for a tale I will weave,
Of flowers and foliage that tease and deceive.
In a world made of colors, they plot and they scheme,
While the wise old oak snoozes away in a dream.

There's Benny the daisy, with petals so bright,
Always claiming he's got the best view of light.
But the humble old fern, resting low on the ground,
Secretly giggles, for his wisdom's profound.

"You think you're the star?" says a cheeky young weed,
"With your flashy display, it's attention you plead!
But when storms come a-blowing, and winds start to howl,
We'll thrive in the shadows, under nature's growl!"

So next time you stumble on blooms dressed in gleam,
Just know there's a story, hidden within their dream.
For every bright petal, with its vainglory scheme,
There's a quirky old plant with a powerful beam!

Between Lifetimes of Blooms

In a garden of whimsy, time twists and bends,
Where petals can chatter and laughter transcends.
"I was once a grand rose, with a scent of delight,
Now I'm this odd shrub, and oh what a fright!"

A geranium snickered, "Oh don't be so blue,
We all have our phases, it's just what we do.
Yesterday's glam, is today's tangled mess,
But who needs perfection? I'll take sassiness!"

With each season's change, they sprouted new quirks,
From colorful buds, to shy little quirks.
The butterfly giggled, as she flitted about,
"Life's just a cycle, let's dance and not pout!"

So remember in gardens, we all have our days,
Where we bloom, and we wither, in fascinating ways.
Celebrate each phase, with a giggle and cheer,
For life's just a party, let's keep it sincere!

In Search of Solitude

In a garden lush and bright,
I sought some peace and light.
But bees were buzzing all around,
Their chatter was a lively sound.

I hid behind a giant leaf,
Hoping to escape my grief.
But butterflies, they found me fast,
And flitted by, a colorful cast.

I thought a rock would do the trick,
But ants piled up, oh what a kick!
They marched in lines, a comical sight,
My solitude turned into a fight.

As I ran off, what a jest!
Nature's chaos never lets you rest.
In search of peace, I found pure glee,
Dance of critters surrounding me.

Watcher of the Flora

I perched upon a garden chair,
To watch the flowers, unaware.
A daisy sneezed, I stifled a laugh,
As pollen flew, what a gaffe!

The roses blushed, their petals wide,
They giggled with the summer tide.
The tulips danced, so bold and bright,
While I clapped hands in pure delight.

A squirrel jumped, a cheeky chap,
I waved at him, he took a nap.
The lilies whispered, secrets deep,
All flowering friends, a laugh to keep.

Nature's jesters, every hue,
Playing tricks, and pulling through.
I sat back, let joy unfold,
In a world of blooms, a story told.

Petals in the Sunlight

Petals shimmer, gleam, and glow,
In sunlight's warm, delightful show.
I tried to catch one, oh what fun,
But it danced away, just like a pun.

A bumblebee was close behind,
In search of nectar, sweet and kind.
He buzzed and hopped, a merry chase,
While I tumbled, fell on my face.

The daisies chuckled, one by one,
As I attempted to leap and run.
They swayed and swirled, a gentle tease,
Laughter floated on the breeze.

But with a smile, I stood up tall,
For slipping in petals, was worth it all.
A sunlight laugh in bloom's embrace,
Nature's joy, a perfect place.

A Glimpse into Grace

In the garden, miracles dance,
Each flower sways as if in a trance.
A clumsy bee, with swirling flight,
Buzzed by me, what a comical sight!

The sunflowers turned, all in a row,
With necks so long, they put on a show.
I chuckled loud, their faces bright,
Waving 'hello' in pure delight.

A ladybug, in polka dots,
Waddled over, it surely plots.
With a wink, it strolled right past,
I wondered if it'd be the last.

With petals bright and laughter clear,
Nature's humor draws us near.
A glimpse of grace in bloom today,
In a funny dance, it leads the way.

Butterfly's Confidant

In a garden where colors dance and sway,
A butterfly whispered her secrets each day.
She giggled at flowers, oh what a sight,
Claimed they wore dresses, quite snug and tight.

With petals like capes, they flaunted their style,
She'd flutter around, her charm none could rile.
"Look at that bloom, it's trying too hard!"
She chuckled and twirled, free of any guard.

The bees buzzed with envy, thought her a show,
While daisies stood tall, proudly putting on a glow.
With each little jest, laughter filled the air,
In this silly world, who could dare compare?

And when the sun dropped, she still felt alive,
Practicing poses, it made her thrive.
"Tomorrow I'll charm them, just wait and see!"
With dreams and big giggles, she flew off with glee.

The Essence of Stillness

In a pot snug and round, sat a flower so shy,
Wishing for company as butterflies passed by.
She'd murmur to raindrops, they listened real close,
Whispering tales of the garden across.

"Oh darling, it's quiet, come dance on my leaves!"
Inviting her friends with a voice that deceives.
With roots so entrenched, she pondered her fate,
"Is it too late for me to be great?"

A snail made her laugh with his slow, silly crawl,
"Life's not in a hurry," he'd sing with a drawl.
She'd sway to his rhythm, feeling the groove,
The essence of stillness, a calming move.

The wind tickled petals, brushed softly aside,
"Oh, you cheeky breeze! You can't take my pride!"
As the cosmos agreed, her confidence grew,
In the midst of her stillness, excitement broke through.

Unveiled Mystique

Beneath the moonlight, a bud held its grin,
Wondering why that old frog jumped in.
"Why hide in the shadows? Come join in my fun!"
She called to the critters, from bird to the bun.

With petals like secrets, she promised a show,
"Once I bloom big, just wait for the glow!"
But the fireflies laughed, "This isn't no race,"
As they zoomed in tight circles around the bright space.

She opened her heart when the night reached its peak,
And frogs brought their croaks, looking rather chic.
"Darling, we'll dance, your reveal is grand!"
With a twirl and a wink, they joined hand-in-hand.

A shimmery night where laughter held sway,
Even snails joined the line, grooving away.
With each little wiggle, she learned to embrace,
In her unveiled mystique, they all found their place.

Guardian of Orchid Dreams

In a realm where petals spun tales far and wide,
Lived a guardian figure, in colors he'd hide.
His job was to watch, with a humorous flair,
Every whim and giggle, caught floatin' in air.

With a straw hat upon, he sipped dew like tea,
Joke-telling squirrels danced under the tree.
"Now don't you be shy, bloom bright for the crew,
Let's get this party hopping, there's fun things to do!"

A vision of chaos, yet harmony thrived,
As breezes and blooms in laughter arrived.
The daisies would twirl, while petunias swayed,
Under watchful old eyes, their joys never strayed.

With every sweet giggle, each flower would bloom,
Under the warm rays, they banished all gloom.
Guardian of laughter, he raised up his cup,
"Here's to the petals, let's drink from the pup!"

Serendipity Among Stems

In a garden, blooms take flight,
A squirrel juggles, what a sight!
Petals giggle, roots do dance,
While bees bring joy, a buzzing chance.

Sunlight tickles every leaf,
While frogs make puns, oh, what a thief!
Butterflies laugh, they flutter near,
Promising nectar with their cheer.

Dancing shadows, colors clash,
A bumblebee with a mustache!
Hilarious mishaps by the pond,
Where daisies bloom and tails respond.

Who knew that nature could be bright?
With steamy romances in daylight!
A playful twist in every bend,
In this garden, joy won't end.

The Orchid's Quietude

In a pot, silence weighs a ton,
An orchid whispers, 'You're not fun!'
While ants march in a little line,
Sipping dew, feeling divine.

The sun peeks, 'Hey, what's the fuss?'
While slugs slide by without a rush.
An antelope watching, eyes so wide,
As a snail wins the slow race with pride.

Petals blush as breezes tease,
While frogs croak jokes with such great ease.
'Why don't flowers ever get lost?'
'They follow the sun, no matter the cost!'

Even shadows giggle at night,
When moonbeams dance in soft twilight.
In this stillness, joy does bloom,
With laughter rising, dispelling gloom.

Fascination in Flora

A cactus pricks with a little grin,
'Don't come too close, or you'll spin!'
But daisies' charm will hold you near,
With petals bright and laughter clear.

In the garden, a flower fights,
With weeds and grasses for silly rights.
'Not today,' shouts a sunflower bold,
As pansies gossip, secrets unfold.

Hummingbirds flaunt their tiny flair,
Competing for nectar with flashy air.
'Too sweet to handle!' they chirp and sway,
While petals laugh at their ballet.

When tulips trip on the muddy floor,
They all just chuckle and ask for more.
In this bloom-filled, bustling bazaar,
Joy springs forth, like a bright shooting star.

When Pollinators Meet

A bee in stripes, oh what a sight,
Buzzing loudly with all its might.
Wasp joins in, with a funky dance,
Pollinating in such a trance.

The dragonfly with wings so bright,
Swoops and zooms, a true delight.
They gather 'round for a little chat,
'Who's got the best nectar? Now, how 'bout that?'

Flowers party, petals flair,
While a butterfly steals the air.
'Let's sip sweet nectar till we're too full!'
They giggle and laugh, making a hullabaloo.

When evening falls, their dance concludes,
With tired whispers and friendly moods.
Pollinators smile, they've done their part,
In this garden, they fill the heart.

Treading Lightly on Fragile Ground

In jungles deep, with laughter loud,
I tiptoe soft, beneath the cloud.
Each step I take, a dance on air,
To find the blooms beyond compare.

The leaves they whisper secrets old,
Of shenanigans, both brave and bold.
With every stumble, giggles flow,
Such fragile ground, but where's the show?

My friends all laugh, a silly crew,
With muddy shoes, what can we do?
Yet through the muck, we spot the hues,
Of blooms that wear the wildest shoes.

So here I tread, both light and free,
In nature's court, where I decree:
With humor high and spirits bright,
We blend with blooms, what a delight!

The Enigmatic Orchid

Oh, what a character it seems,
This flower dressed in vibrant dreams.
With petals ruffled, looking sly,
It winks at me, oh my, oh my!

In shades of purple, pink, and green,
A floral jester, quite the queen.
It giggles softly in the breeze,
A playful charm that aims to please.

I bring a friend to share the view,
We both just laugh at what it grew.
With roots held tight, it shows off flair,
Yet dares us to just stop and stare.

So here we stand, in awe and glee,
At nature's joke, can you see me?
A riddle wrapped in petals fine,
An enigma that's divine, divine!

Nature's Painted Heirlooms

In sunlight bright, the colors gleam,
Nature's brush strokes make us beam.
A tapestry upon the ground,
With artistry that knows no bound.

Each petal tells a tale so grand,
Of paint that splashes on the land.
With every hue, there's laughter near,
As blooms unveil their quirky cheer.

Old leaves giggle, rich with lore,
Of garden antics, tales to score.
They swirl and twirl in gentle grace,
Whilst flowers chuckle, take their place.

So when you roam through vibrant lands,
Embrace the joy that nature brands.
For laughter blooms where colors play,
In every petal, come what may!

Petal by Petal

Oh, how they flutter, those delicate dreams,
Unruly dancers, bursting at the seams.
Petal by petal, they sway with glee,
Playing hide and seek, just wait and see!

They pop and twirl on their slender stalks,
These floral jesters, oh what a hoax!
With every breeze, they giggle and spin,
Welcoming all, come join the din!

Nature's whoopee cushions, full of flair,
Contorting in laughter, with style to spare.
In gardens bright, the fun's not planned,
Just leave your worries and take a stand.

So come along, and dance with the blooms,
In their silly world where laughter looms.
Petal by petal, we find delight,
In nature's whimsy, everything's right!

Beneath the Canopy of Enchantment

In a garden where laughter sways,
Petals giggle in sunny rays,
Butterflies dance like it's a race,
Trying to keep up with their grace.

A squirrel stole a bloom for fun,
Claiming it's a crown, he's won,
While ladybugs cheer its style,
Adorning his head with a smile.

The bees buzz in a silly tune,
As flowers sway like a cartoon,
Each bloom dons a funny hat,
Making all the critters chat.

Underneath this vibrant scene,
Joy and laughter reign supreme,
With petals that wink and tease,
Nature's fun, a playful breeze.

Awakening the Hidden Blooms

In the quiet of dawn's soft light,
Flowers yawn, all snug and tight,
A daisy sneezes, 'Ah-choo!'
And sunflowers chuckle, 'How rude of you!'

Tulips play peek-a-boo with the sun,
While violets giggle, oh what fun!
In a world where blooms slyly scheme,
Dreaming up the wildest dream.

A curious bee with a cap and gown,
Dutifully buzzes and then swoops down,
"Excuse my friends, let's start the show,
Let's see how many seeds we can throw!"

As blossoms stir in morning's blush,
Laughter echoes in the rush,
With each petal stretching wide,
Awakening joy, no need to hide.

Whispers Among Petals

In a realm where colors play,
Petals gossip all the day,
"Oh darling, did you see that bee?
Such a fashionista, wild and free!"

Lavender laughs, a secret shared,
While roses blush, slightly scared,
Dancing daisies join the fun,
Twirling around in the sun.

"Did you know about that shady shrub?
He tries to be cool, but he's just a grub!"
The orchids roll their eyes in jest,
Claiming they hold the title, 'Best Dressed.'

Each flower has a tale to tell,
Whispers of joy, they weave so well,
Among the petals, stories bloom,
Creating laughter, breaking gloom.

Gaze of the Bloom

A sunflower winks at the sky,
"Why don't clouds float by and fly?"
Petals giggle at their sight,
Making clouds blush, oh what a fright!

A blossom darts with cheeky flair,
Trying to catch a fragrant air,
"Watch me twirl!" it shouts with glee,
As bees buzz along, "Oh, look at me!"

A violets' dance is quite the scene,
Shaking its leaves in shades of green,
With every sway and every move,
It creates a laughter groove.

So come and gaze, don't just glance,
In this garden, blooms will prance,
With humor-filled trails, they'll charm,
Nature's joy spreads, no alarm.

Petal Trails

In a garden bright, where petals play,
A sneaky bee buzzed his way.
"Try my nectar, it's oh so sweet!"
Said the flower, with a friendly greet.

The petals danced with a silly spin,
A squirrel peeked in with a cheeky grin.
"Do you have snacks? Or just this bloom?"
The flowers giggled, spreading the room!

A butterfly flapped with a loud cheer,
"I'm not late, I just like to veer!"
With vibrant hues, they twirled in glee,
Making laughter amongst the trees.

Just leaves and stems in a merry war,
Waging fun like never before!
Petal trails lead to a happy phase,
Nature's jokes bring sunny days.

Eavesdropping on Nature

Hush now, listen, the trees have much
Their branches gossip like friends at lunch.
A rustle here, a whisper there,
"Oh my, did you see her hair?"

The bees are buzzing, plotting their plans,
"Who wore it best? The roses or pans?"
Nature's tales with a twist of fun,
Making mischief under the sun.

A frog croaked loud, "I'm the best crooner!"
While birds agreed, "He's a real gooner!"
They giggled and chirped till the daylight ceased,
Nature's comedy never released!

As shadows danced, secrets flew,
A world of laughter hidden from view.
Eavesdropping on life, what a delight,
Nature's humor shines through the night!

The Secret Keeper's Diary

In the garden, a diary sits tight,
Filled with secrets, quite the sight!
"Today I saw a squirrel in socks,
Prancing about like a bearded ox!"

Petals turned pages with blossoms galore,
"Do you think they look at us, or ignore?"
The daisies laughed, while roses sighed,
"What a wild world, with secrets to hide!"

A ladybug scribbled a story or two,
Of grand adventures, and trouble anew.
"Hiding from rain, I danced with a bee,
Swapping tales of nectar, quite carefree!"

The diary giggled, under moonlight bright,
With pages fluttering, such pure delight!
Hidden murmurs in botanical land,
Nature's gossip, simply unplanned!

Senses of the Botanist

A botanist sniffed with a curious nose,
"Hmm, this flower, it echoes or glows!"
When petals are painted with colors so bold,
They tickled his senses, both lively and cold.

He poked and he prodded, with a gentle hand,
"Is this a fragrance, or just dirt on the land?"
The plants just chuckled, in tones quite spry,
"Don't worry, dear friend, we're just passing by!"

A splash of pollen, a dab on his cheek,
"Goodness, dear flowers, you play hide and seek!"
His notebook filled with laughter and joy,
As he surveyed blooms, each one a ploy.

"Frog or a flower? What's on today's chart?"
He scribbled with wonder, "Nature's an art!"
With senses a-buzzing, he danced all around,
In the world of flowers, hilarity found!

Beyond the Garden Gate

In the garden, things grow wild,
The cat thinks it's a sprawling child.
Bees buzz in a frantic dance,
While worms plot their slimy romance.

Sun shines down with a cheeky grin,
Plants gossip about where they've been.
Sneaky squirrels steal the show,
While the roses just sit and glow.

A hat gets lifted by a breeze,
Tangled in the branches, oh, the tease!
Tulips chuckle, they seem so proud,
"Look at us!" they say, and laugh out loud.

We laugh at nature's silly tricks,
Garden chaos always picks.
Behind the gate, a riot thrives,
Where flowers dance and laughter jives.

Enigma of Green

In a sea of leaves, who can find,
A plant that's truly one of a kind?
Cacti wear hats, how odd indeed,
While ferns whisper secrets, take heed!

Moss plots to smother a lonely stone,
As lilies sing soft, their roots have grown.
What's the secret of this vibrant hue?
Do plants have parties, if only we knew?

In the shadows, a gnome takes a nap,
Wakes up to find leaves on his cap.
"Who invited you?" he states with a frown,
As daisies giggle and sway all around.

The sun tickles leaves, making them sway,
While squirrels chase their acorn buffet.
In this green world of laughter and fun,
Each plant holds a joke, just for everyone.

In the Company of Blooms

Daisies walk in their polka-dot shoes,
Chasing flies while wearing their hues.
Tulips whisper pass-it-on gossip,
While peonies boast, "Come on, let's hop!"

The violets joke, "We're shy, it's true,"
Yet bold under sun, they dance in a queue.
Carnations claim they smell the best,
While daisies play games—who would have guessed?

Sunflowers stretch, they're making a scene,
"Why can't you all be tall like me?"
But down low, the pansies smirk with delight,
"We're colorful too, try us tonight!"

In this garden, the soggy weeds lie,
With dreams of being tall, oh so shy.
But amongst the blooms, there's laughter and cheer,
A garden party, everyone's here!

Unfolding Perceptions

Each petal's fold hides tales so strange,
Like roses dreaming of a cosmetic change.
Tulips complain they're stuck in a row,
Unaware that the weeds steal the show!

In the breeze, the daisies sway,
Murmuring secrets about the day.
"What if we wore shoes, how would we be?"
"Fancy, for sure! Just wait and see!"

The marigolds paint the scene so bright,
While violets ponder their contribution to light.
But nature's wild humor spills out so free,
With every flower in on the spree!

Every bud brings laughter by design,
In this garden of quirks, all is divine.
So here's to blooms, in shades galore,
Let's raise a laugh, we could always use more!

Wandering Among Whispers

In gardens where secrets bloom,
An ant wears shades, consumes the gloom.
A butterfly, with gossip to share,
Giggles soft, floating in the air.

A snail recites jokes with flair,
While flowerpots become a fair.
Daisies dance, wearing bright hats,
And cats think they're guardians of chats.

The breeze joins in, it's quite the laugh,
As weeds show off their wiggly path.
In every nook, fun does reside,
Among the flora, jokes can't hide.

With crayons made of petals wide,
They sketch a world where laughter's tied.
Watch out for humor, it sneaks in close,
In this garden, joy is gross!

Petals' Silent Stories

Each petal hides a tale so sly,
Of whispers shared 'neath the blue sky.
A daisy dreams of being a crown,
While violets pout, feeling quite down.

A tulip's crush on a passing breeze,
In secret loves, they flaunt with ease.
Whirligigs spin, with tales they weave,
As snickers bloom, it's hard to leave.

Laughter echoes from leafy nooks,
The roses write their own funny books.
They giggle at bees who misplace their stride,
In this quiet realm, joy does not hide.

Snippets of humor, soft and light,
In nature's backdrop, pure delight.
Every bloom's giggle paints the air,
With silent stories, laughter's everywhere.

Conversations in the Garden

Two petunias gossip in the sun,
Sharing tales, oh, what fun!
An old toad croaks in the back,
Hopping in with a witty smack.

"Did you hear what the fern just said?"
With roots entwined, they laugh instead.
A ladybug rolls her eyes and sighs,
While lilacs plot to claim the skies.

Grass blades sway to the comedy tune,
A flower race 'neath the bright moon.
Plants exchange jokes, they burst with glee,
As nature's own comedy set sets free.

By the fence, a worm attempts to jive,
With moves so silly, it's no surprise.
In this green world where laughter reigns,
The dialogues of laughter break the chains.

Luminance in the Shade

In shaded spots, the chatter's bright,
Where shadows spill with pure delight.
Sassy leaves and petals tease,
With whispers carried by the breeze.

A lazy cat sprawls, plays the fool,
While blossoms engage in a playful duel.
Glorious giggles from hidden nooks,
As creeping vines steal all the looks.

Beneath tall trees, stories intertwine,
Where every rustle hints at a sign.
The sun sneaks through, plays peek-a-boo,
Only to trip on laughing dew.

From night to day, hilarity thrives,
With every bloom, joy survives.
A garden alive with humorous grace,
In quiet corners, mischief finds its space.

Vistas of Verdant Wonder

In gardens bright where colors clash,
A flower dressed in green and sash.
It winks and nods, a cheeky thing,
While bees around it dance and sing.

With petals wide and charm so grand,
It sways like it just joined a band.
A sunny smile, a grassy throne,
It claims the world, yet sits alone.

A curious bud with secrets deep,
In daytime's light, we stir from sleep.
It giggles softly, blushing red,
As butterflies perch on its head.

Oh! What a sight, this floral jest,
Nature's prankster, always dressed best.
In every bloom, a tale unfolds,
In vivid green, this fun it holds.

Embracing Serenity

Deep in the leaves where whispers creep,
The flowers plot while others sleep.
With gentle laughs and breezy cheer,
They share their thoughts that only they hear.

A lovely joke upon the breeze,
Each bloom sways softly, aiming to please.
Petals flutter with giddy glee,
Nature's giggle floats, wild and free.

As sunlight paints a perfect hue,
The jovial roots hold stories true.
In every sigh of fragrant air,
Life's little pranks put stress to despair.

This tranquil space of green delight,
Where flowers joke from dawn 'til night.
With every glance, their humor shines,
In every petal, laughter aligns.

Stories Written in Scent

In fragrant tales that flutter by,
Each flower holds a wink, a sigh.
With hints of laughter in the air,
Petals tease with jests to share.

Leaves rustle softly, tell their lore,
Whisking tales from core to core.
Tales of bees, of sunlit days,
Each scent a giggle, nature plays.

As perfumes mingle, chuckles grow,
In every breeze, a smile will flow.
Whiffs of joy twist through the trees,
Nature's sweet sense of humor's keys.

These fragrant whispers through the glade,
A comic script in bloom displayed.
As scents unveil their funny quirks,
In every whiff, the laughter lurks.

A Canvas of Nature's Artistry

In every color, a merry dance,
Petals prance like they're in a trance.
Dancing amidst the paint so bright,
Nature's palette, pure delight.

With polka dots and stripes alive,
Each flower boasts, "Look how I thrive!"
A laugh or two spins on the breeze,
As art takes root among the trees.

Creativity blooms, wild and free,
In the garden's gentle gallery.
With daffodils in fancy hats,
Stirring mischief, how time flies! That's.

A canvas bright with laughter's glow,
Where nature's brush strokes ebb and flow.
In every bloom, a tale doth spin,
A funny masterpiece to begin.

Between Sun and Soil

In the garden, what a scene,
Dancing beetles, a silly routine.
Sunflowers gossip, tall and proud,
While daisies giggle, in the crowd.

Worms in a tie, digging down deep,
Plotting their plans, secrets to keep.
Roots doing yoga, stretching so wide,
While ants throw a party, not a soul to hide.

Frogs croak out some cheesy tunes,
As crickets leap under cartoon moons.
Bees wear hats, buzzing off track,
Spreading the news, "Hey, come back!"

Through sun and soil, chaos reigns,
Nature chuckles amid its gains.
With every twist, and every turn,
The garden teaches—let's laugh and learn!

Unfolding Layers of Elegance

Petals peek out, soft and shy,
Wearing colors that catch the eye.
A bouquet of laughter, blooms in disguise,
Who knew flowers had such wise eyes?

Each bud a riddle, fragrant and bold,
With stories of sunlight, waiting to be told.
Butterflies shimmy, in quite the frock,
As blossoms play dress-up, what a shock!

Bees must be stylists, buzzing around,
With pollen tips, they're fashion-bound.
Who knew that nature had such flair?
With petals of velvet, elegance rare!

As layers unfold, humor takes flight,
In the garden of laughter, everything's right.
Springtime's delight, a whimsical sight,
Nature's own jesters, in the soft light.

An Ode to Resilience

In the crack of concrete, blooms pop through,
Defying the odds, who knew they'd do?
A daisy in battle, with a messenger's flair,
"Take that, stony path! I really don't care!"

Roses and thorns, a comical mix,
What's with the drama? Oh, these nature tricks!
Twirling in storms, like it's a dance,
Every gust sung, gives them a chance.

A cactus in winter, wearing a grin,
"Here's to survival; let the fun begin!"
With spikes like armor and style to boot,
Every critter thinks, "That's quite a hoot!"

So here's to green warriors, standing so tall,
With roots like legends, they won't let us fall.
In the face of chaos, they throw up their hands,
And giggle in silence, as resilience stands.

Mysteries of the Wild Bloom

In the wild, where secrets sway,
Colors tumble, come what may.
What's that giggling, in the breeze?
A chorus of blooms, with hearts that tease!

Ferns whisper stories, ancient and sly,
"Why don't you dance?" they softly reply.
With petals as secrets, unfolding their tricks,
Nature's own jesters, full of quick quips.

Beetles put on their best tap shoes,
As flowers recite their favorite blues.
They throw in some jazz, just for a laugh,
While bumblebees lead the whole dance path!

In tangled vines and blossoms' embrace,
Each twist brings a smile, a playful trace.
From the wild blooms, laughter will rise,
In the garden of joy, where mystery lies.

Nature's Quiet Watcher

In the garden, a sneaky spy,
Watches petals dance and fly.
With a wink and a funny grin,
Waiting for bees to drop and spin.

A butterfly lands, claims its throne,
Sipping nectar like it's its own.
But the watcher giggles, can't deny,
It's just a flower, oh my, oh my!

Bees misbehave, they bump and jive,
Think they're stars, so cool, alive.
Oh, what a show, they buzz and zoom,
In nature's hall, they've found their room.

Under sunbeams, a leaf will sway,
Sipping sunlight day by day.
And the watcher, with eyes so wide,
Just laughs at the antics that they've tried.

Reflections in the Orchid's Eye

In a puddle near the bloom,
A subtle splash, it starts to zoom.
Critters shimmy by the hue,
Nature's party just for two.

Mirror mirror, who's the fairest?
A bee says, "Me! I'm the rarest!"
But the orchid rolls its petals tight,
"Might want to check your sense of sight!"

A bug takes a fancy beetle dance,
But slips and falls—oh, what a chance!
The flowers laugh, they cannot hide,
As chaos reigns, they swell with pride.

In the twilight, as starlight falls,
A shimmering glow across the walls.
The watcher snickers at the scene,
In nature's hall of vivid green.

The Hidden Sanctuary

Deep in the jungle, oh so sly,
Lurks a pocket where giggles lie.
A secret fest for flowers bright,
Where petals gossip, day and night.

Frogs croak jokes that make them laugh,
While ladybugs sign autographs.
A snail slides in, says, "I'm a star!"
But the petals don't agree by far!

"Is that a weed?" a flower asked,
Its neighbor chuckled, "What a task!"
With petals folded, they conspire,
To keep the scene just truly dire.

In hidden paths, the antics swirl,
Leaves of laughter start to twirl.
The sanctuary keeps its cheer,
For every bloom is welcome here!

Colorful Reverie

A splash of yellow, a hint of pink,
In this sea of colors, one's got to blink.
A parrot squawks with glee and flair,
"Is that your lipstick? Better share!"

The orchids giggle as colors clash,
Petals swirling like a fast dance dash.
"Hey, purple, you're looking quite bold!"
"Just trying to keep the stories told!"

A wandering bug joins the fun,
Zooming 'round like it's in the sun.
"Catch me if you can!" it pleads,
But flowers know their stealthy beads.

As night draws near, the laughter fades,
In hues of twilight, a shift pervades.
But in this garden, laughter stays,
For joy in blooms will always blaze.

Delicate Echoes of Growth

In a pot of dirt, she takes her stand,
Roots wriggle like they're in a band.
With petals waving at the bee,
"Hey, what's buzzing? Come dance with me!"

Sunlight drips from the leafy crown,
"Why you frowning, girl? Don't drown!"
The gardener's laughter spills on the floor,
"Your blooms are wacky, but oh, give more!"

Potted plants gossip in colorful tones,
"Did you see that? She's got quite the drones!"
They share stories of mysterious blooms,
Absurd little tales of gardening Zooms.

A ladybug struts with unmatched flair,
"Are you a flower? Or just caught in air?"
Echoes of giggles float on the breeze,
While petals nod in hilarious tease.

Observations from the Edge

Peering through petals, a curious sight,
"Why's that leaf wearing glasses, so bright?"
With a chuckle, the observer leans close,
"Is that fashion, or just a vegetable dose?"

Flirting with birds, the blooms swear and spin,
"Do you think he likes me? Let's begin!"
One bloom blushes, then falls in a swoon,
"Stop! You might scare him off too soon!"

They laugh at the sun, who's a bit too bold,
"Throw on a hat, your rays are too cold!"
While shadows create the best kind of shade,
Together they joke in the flower parade.

From the edge of the garden, giggles take flight,
With potting soil dreams and pollen in sight.
A snapshot of joy, in this fragrant nook,
Just watch out for squirrels—they steal the good look!

Seasons of an Orchid

Springtime arrives with a bouncy tap,
"Hey guys! Ready for a twirling nap?"
Buds bounce with laughter, bright and bold,
Twirling around, like a classic hold.

Summer rolls in with a cheeky grin,
"Look at me shine! Where do I begin?"
Leaves high-five the breeze, rustle away,
"Let's have a picnic, let's seize the day!"

Autumn slips in with a clumsy shake,
"Whoa there! Did you see that crazy rake?"
With colors that giggle, they dance in delight,
Who knew leaves could waltz through the night?

Winter arrives, and they cozy in beds,
With blankets of frost covering their heads.
They tell silly stories of seasons gone by,
"Hey, did you know, we can't even fly?"

Dreams through the Vibrant Veil

A veil of petals sways with a song,
"Do we belong, or are we wrong?"
Dreams float around in a colorful spree,
"Let's paint the world, just you and me!"

Waking up grumpy, a bud with a frown,
"Can someone please help me wear this crown?"
A friend replies with a wink and a tease,
"Just add some sparkle! Say cheese, oh please!"

Through hues of laughter, they concoct a plan,
"To play hide-and-seek with the tallest man!"
Their giggles echo through the garden so wide,
Filling the air with adventures inside.

A dance under moonlight, a whimsical sway,
While dreams softly whisper — come join the play!
In vibrant veils, with humor to spare,
A garden of joy, floating high in the air.

Observations Under Canopy

Under a leafy dome, I spy,
A dainty flower, oh my!
It winks at me with petals bright,
As if to say, 'I'm quite the sight.'

With bees buzzing like a band,
I laugh at nature's careful plan.
They dance around, a sweet ballet,
While I just munch on my parfait.

A frog croaks out a silly tune,
He thinks he's quite the handsome croon.
But with that face and bulgy eyes,
I'm not convinced, I just disguise.

I take my notes, a pen in hand,
While vines reach out, they've got a brand.
Each twist and turn, nature's plot,
Who knew fun bloomed in this hot spot?

Blooming Observations

In the garden, a sight so grand,
A flower's dance, I can't quite stand.
It sways and giggles in the breeze,
Am I the joke? I start to freeze.

Petals bright like circus clothes,
They laugh at me — or so it goes.
With colors that just beg to tease,
Somehow they're more than just a tease.

While daisies stare with puzzled looks,
I ponder life and garden books.
Why bloom in pink when blue ignites?
These flowers love to have their fights.

The sun comes down, the shadows play,
They know the jokes, I can't convey.
With a giggle, I stroll away,
A blooming show without delay.

Camouflage of Beauty

In the jungle, colors blend,
A sneaky bloom, it loves to pretend.
It hides among the leafy green,
'I'm a leaf!' says it, quite unseen.

But wait, a flash of color bright,
It's not a leaf, what a sight!
With butterflies playing peek-a-boo,
I can't help but join the ruse too.

A chameleon in flower guise,
Gloating there, it rolls its eyes.
Who knew that petals could deceive,
A garden full of tricks to weave?

So I tiptoe in this botanical charade,
Where beauty's wrapped in leafy parade.
Nature's tricksters, full of fun,
A game of hide and seek has begun!

Symphony of Shades

In a world where colors clash,
A luscious shade makes quite a splash.
With reds and yellows on parade,
A harmony that won't soon fade.

The blues are cool, so laid-back too,
They subtly strut, a chill adieu.
While violets hum a jazzy tune,
I tap my feet beneath the moon.

Then comes a rogue in orange and pink,
A burst of laughter that makes one think.
In nature's show, it's quite the prize,
A carnival wrapped in shocking guise.

So join the waltz of petals bright,
Where every hue is pure delight.
With sunlight glances, watch them sway,
In this playful symphony today.

Dance of the Delicate

In the garden where petals prance,
Dancing flowers take a chance.
They sway and spin in breezy play,
While bees buzz round without delay.

A dandelion tried to join the show,
But tripped on roots, oh what a blow!
The irises laughed, a vibrant cheer,
"Stick to the ground, it's safer, dear!"

Tulips twirled, in swirls so fair,
While roses tossed their fragrant hair.
Each blossom had a step to teach,
In this wild waltz, no hearts to breach.

With every twirl and giggling spray,
They found their joy in the sun's bright ray.
A parade of colors bright and bold,
Their laughter echoed, a story told.

Elusive Fragrance

Beneath the blooms, a scent so sly,
A whiff of trouble floating high.
With noses twitching, bees did chase,
The perfume spritzed all over the place!

Tulip tried to play a prank,
With a sprout of mint, it sparked a flank.
"Smell this!" she beckoned, oh what fun,
But the bees just buzzed and promptly spun.

An elder rose, with wisdom rife,
Said, "Avoid the stench, it's full of strife!"
While daisies giggled, hardly shy,
"Just let it go, and don't ask why!"

Yet in this chaos, scents did meld,
Creating perfumes, nature held.
A symphony sweet, a fragrant tease,
In laughter's wake, all blooms at ease.

Garden of Gossamer Dreams

In a corner of whimsy, dreams take flight,
Petals whisper secrets, oh what a sight!
A ladybug grins with polka-dot cheer,
Sipping dew drops with a pint of beer.

The sunflowers stretch, all tall and proud,
Making poses for the wandering crowd.
A bumblebee stumbles, lost in the fray,
Roaring with laughter, buzzing away!

A butterfly flutters, with gossamer wings,
Joining the party, oh what joy it brings!
With a flutter and dance, they twirl in delight,
Creating a carnival, morning to night.

So in this garden, dreams intertwine,
With laughter and antics, all things align.
Nature's stage set with colors so bright,
A whimsical world, full of delight!

In the Shadow of Lush Leaves

Under foliage thick, where secrets hide,
Comes a snail that's quite full of pride.
He slides on by, with a wink and a grin,
"Why rush the day when you can just spin?"

While shadows dance under tangled vines,
A frog croaks jokes, tossing witty lines.
"Why leap for bugs? Just lounge and gloat,
Who needs a meal when you've got a moat?"

An umbrella plant opens wide,
As fairies giggle and softly glide.
With mischievous looks, they twirl round the shade,
Tossing tiny water drops like a cascade.

Among the leaves, this circus continues,
With banter and laughter in nature's venues.
Every critter joins in the jest,
In the shadowy realm, it's laughter's quest!

The Vigilant Heart

In gardens rich with blooms so bright,
A bug decided to take flight.
With nectar sweet, it spun around,
The flower laughed, without a sound.

A bee buzzed in, its dance was grand,
With pollen stuck to every hand.
It slipped and tripped, what a ballet,
As petals giggled, come what may.

A curious bird, with eyes so wide,
Peeked in the petals, there to hide.
But oh, a sneeze! It startled all,
And petals blushed, it felt so small.

In shady spots, their mischief thrives,
These plants ensure their humors thrive.
With every bloom and every twist,
Nature chuckles, can't be missed.

Echoed Beauty Beneath

A leafy whisper in the breeze,
Creeping vines tease with such ease.
A ladybug in red attire,
Sipped morning dew, her heart afire.

The sunbeams played, a silly game,
As shadows danced, they called her name.
A thumble down, she tumbled bright,
Amidst the laughter, pure delight.

Petals fluttered, quick and sly,
While buzzing bees would hover by.
"Catch me if you can!" they sang,
As petals giggled, joy clangs.

No finest art can capture true,
The jest of colors in the blue.
With every bloom, a laugh unseen,
Nature's chuckle beneath the green.

Caress of the Orchid's Soul

Upon a stem, a party grows,
With polka dots and fancied hose.
The orchids wink, a sly affair,
In colors bold, they mock the air.

They spread their petals, wide and bright,
With glances sweet – a true delight.
A squirrel peeked; then slipped, oh dear!
Right into blooms, it faced the cheer.

Pollen rain down, a sneaky trap,
"Join the fun!" they giggle and clap.
But little feet got stuck in dew,
And laughed away the morning hue.

With sunny days and starlit nights,
These flowers play in colors' lights.
Each bloom a smile, a cheeky jest,
Together in joy, they're truly blessed.

Portraits of Nature's Artistry

A stroke of green, a splash of hue,
In gardens bright, that's how they grew.
With petals bold, but stems so shy,
They wink and giggle as you pass by.

The petals chat, a gossip spree,
"Did you hear? The bug is free!"
A tiny butterfly gives chase,
And laughs ring out, a breezy race.

In nature's frame of vibrant art,
Colorful souls with playful heart.
Each blossom chats with swaying grace,
Creating smiles in their embrace.

A canvas held in sun and shade,
Where dreams of beauty will not fade.
These portraits dance in bright array,
Reminding us to laugh and play.

Glimpses of the World Within

In a garden where secrets sleep,
Tiny petals gossip and peep.
A bug with shades, strutting by,
Claims it's the reason flowers sigh.

Bees spinning tales, quite absurd,
Swapping honey for every word.
A raccoon with a monocle too,
Sips on dew, wearing its best shoe.

Underneath leaves, a snail narrates,
How it caught the gossip of mates.
While frogs debate who'll sing the best,
With croaks that put talent to test.

Laughter mingles with fragrant air,
In this world, free of all care.
Each petal's a page, a tale to tell,
In the wacky garden where all creatures dwell.

Time's Tapestry in Bloom

Tick-tock, the flowers giggle,
While the sun winks and starts to wiggle.
A daisy dons a tiny hat,
Mocking the clock like a cheeky brat.

The tulips dance to an unseen beat,
While daisies argue who has the best seat.
A squirrel leading moves that surprise,
Wearing a headband, oh what a guise!

Time flies past in a flurry of hues,
Tickling petals with colorful views.
Forget-me-nots scribble quick notes,
On how to be the garden's best folks.

Petals racing with clouds up high,
Playing tag as they twirl and fly.
In this ballet of blooms and cheer,
Every second spent, brings laughter near.

Fables of Fragrance

Once a rose, so grand and bright,
Claimed it smelled best, oh what a sight!
But violets, with a wink and a laugh,
Said, 'Your petals are but a fragrant half!'

Lavender chimed in, sweet and bold,
Whispering secrets of scents untold.
'It's not the bloom, it's the laughs we share,
Fragrance isn't just found in the air!'

A lilac huddled, full of glee,
And spun tales of bee's jubilee.
With mischief, each petal spread a word,
Challenging those who had not heard.

A dandelion, full of sass,
Said it too had as much class.
For in every puff, laughter flies,
When seeds embark on merry tries.

Nature's Gentle Reminder

The breeze tickles the blooms, a game of tease,
While petals chatter, making light of ease.
A butterfly with a top hat floats,
Inviting all friends to join on boats.

The daisies argue who'll wear the crown,
While sunflowers laugh with roots in the ground.
A grasshopper croons, a song so sweet,
Reminding us all of life's little beat.

Clouds drift by, making faces with glee,
As if they too join the grassy spree.
Laughter bubbles at the edge of the brook,
While frogs in tuxedos share a good look.

In this dance of life, nature's call,
To find joy in moments, both big and small.
So next time you stroll through a garden's embrace,
Remember to smile—it's a funny place!

www.ingramcontent.com/pod-product-compliance
Lightning Source LLC
Chambersburg PA
CBHW051658160426
43209CB00004B/937